Psalms

HEART TO HEART WITH GOD

Walter C. Kaiser, Jr.

ZondervanPublishingHouse
Grand Rapids, Michigan

A Division of HarperCollins*Publishers*

Psalms: Heart to Heart with God
Copyright © 1995 by Walter C. Kaiser, Jr.

Requests for information should be addressed to:

ZondervanPublishingHouse
Grand Rapids, Michigan 49530

ISBN 13: 978-0-310-49871-1

Cover design by Jeff Sharpton, PAZ Design Group
Cover photograph by William J. Hebert
Interior design by Joe Vriend

Printed in the United States of America

CONTENTS

Great Books of the Bible 5

Introduction: Heart to Heart with God 9

1. Listen and Learn 13
   Psalms 1 and 19

2. God Is King 19
   Psalm 2

3. Praising God's Majesty 25
   Psalms 117 and 100

4. How Great Is Our God? 31
   Psalm 139

5. Worshiping the Holy King of Glory 35
   Psalm 24

6. Praying Out of the Depths of Our Sinfulness 41
   Psalm 130

7. Confessing Our Transgressions 45
   Psalms 51 and 32

8. The Lord Is Present 51
   Psalms 23 and 46

9. On the Edge of Unbelief 55
   Psalm 73

10. Coming to Terms with Time .61
    Psalm 90

11. Standing Beneath the Cross of Jesus 65
    Psalm 22

12. Walking Around Zion 69
    Psalms 48 and 122

Leader's Notes 73

GREAT BOOKS OF THE BIBLE

Every book of the Bible is important, because each one is inspired by God. But certain books draw us to them time and again for their strong encouragement, powerful teaching, and practical wisdom. The Great Books of the Bible Series brings into one collection eight biblical books that distinguish themselves either because of their undisputed excellence or because they are perennial favorites.

The Psalms, with their poetic imagery, help us express our emotions to God and see the myriad ways God works during the best and worst times of our lives. Two books—Proverbs in the Old Testament and James in the New Testament—offer practical wisdom for dealing with the decisions and realities of everyday life. The gospel of John gives us the most intimate and personal view of Jesus, the God-become-man who is Savior and Lord.

Three books are letters written by the apostle Paul. Romans is Paul's masterpiece—the clearest and fullest explanation of the gospel found in Scripture; there we see our world through God's eyes. Philippians shows us how to experience joy when we are under pressure. Ephesians explores the crucial role of the church as a living community, giving us just a little taste of heaven on earth as we seek to serve the Lord.

The series ends where the Bible does—with Revelation, the last book of the Bible, where we glimpse our glorious future, when all things will become new.

Whether you are a new student of God's Word or one who has studied these books many times before, you will find here new insights and fresh perspectives that will make the Bible come alive for you.

The Great Books of the Bible Series is designed to be flexible. You can use the guides in any order. You can use them individually or in a small group or Sunday school class. Some of the guides have six studies; others have as many as thirteen. Moreover, these books help us discover what the Bible says rather than simply telling us the answers. The questions encourage us to think and explore options rather than merely filling in the blanks with one-word answers.

Leader's notes are provided in the back of each guide. They show how to lead a group discussion, provide additional information on questions, and suggest ways to deal with problems that may come up in the discussion. With such helps, someone with little or no experience can lead an effective study.

Suggestions for Individual Study

1. Begin each study with prayer. Ask God to help you understand the passage and to apply it to your life.

2. A good modern translation, such as the *New International Version,* the *New American Standard Bible,* or the *New Revised Standard Version,* will give you the most help. Questions in this guide are based on the *New International Version.*

3. Read and reread the passage(s). You must know what the passage says before you can understand what it means and how it applies to you.

4. Write your answers in the spaces provided in the study guide. This will help you to express clearly your understanding of the passage.

5. Keep a Bible dictionary handy. Use it to look up unfamiliar words, names, or places.

Suggestions for Group Study

1. Come to the study prepared. Careful preparation will greatly enrich your time in group discussion.

2. Be willing to join in the discussion. The leader of the group will not be lecturing, but will encourage people to discuss what they have learned in the passage. Plan to share what God has taught you in your individual study.

3. Stick to the passage being studied. Base your answers on the verses being discussed rather than on outside authorities such as commentaries or your favorite author or speaker.

4. Try to be sensitive to the other members of the group. Listen attentively when they speak, and be affirming whenever you can. This will encourage more hesitant members of the group to participate.

5. Be careful not to dominate the discussion. By all means participate! But allow others to have equal time.

6. If you are the discussion leader, you will find additional suggestions and helpful ideas in the leader's notes at the back of the guide.

HEART TO HEART WITH GOD

Psalms, the longest book in the Bible, is a book of music without notes and prayers without restraint. It contains at one and the same time some of the loftiest notes of praise for our God and some of the lowest sounds of groaning of a heart that is ready to break if it soon does not hear from its Deliverer.

This dual nature of the Psalms can be seen first in its Hebrew title, which means "Praises [to God]." Even though this designation is found in only one psalm superscription (Psalm 145), it is the Hebrew printed title for the whole book. However, a case could be made for titling this book "Prayers," because the doxology given at the end of Book II (Psalm 72:20) says, "This concludes the prayers of David, the son of Jesse." Therefore we will find that studying the book of Psalms is also to enter the school of prayer.

Nearly half of the Psalms are attributed to David, "Israel's singer of songs" or "beloved singer" (2 Samuel 23:1). Fourteen of the seventy-three Psalms ascribed to him carry headings that connect them with events in his life. Other authors of the Psalms include Solomon (two psalms); Moses (one psalm); sons of Korah (twelve); Asaph (twelve); Heman the Ezrahite (one); and Ethan the Ezrahite (one).

The Psalter is structured around five books, which begin respectively at Psalms 1, 42, 73, 90, and 107. Each book appropriately concludes with a doxology. Whether these five books were meant to correspond with the five books of Moses, or with some other such arrangement, is unclear; there is no consensus among biblical scholars. But there are some clear clusters of material. Some of the better known, in addition to those already mentioned, are these:

— Almost all the psalms in Book II prefer to use the name *Elohim* ("God") rather than Yahweh ("LORD");

9

— Books IV and V use *Yahweh* almost without exception; Psalms 93–100 exalt the worldwide kingship of the Lord;
— Psalms 113–118 are the Hallel ("praise") Psalms sung on Passover night;
— Psalms 120–134 are the Psalms of Ascent sung by the pilgrims on their way to celebrate the three annual feasts in Jerusalem;
— The final Hallel Psalms conclude the collection in Psalms 146–150. In addition to the great Davidic collection that embraces most of Books I and II, there are two sets of Davidic psalms in Psalms 108–110 and 138–145.

The Psalms are written in Hebrew poetry, which is quite different from Western forms of poetry. The latter depend, among other things, on rhyme and meter, whereas Hebrew poetry places its emphasis on a balancing of thought and ideas. While there is a general sense of how many words are needed in the half lines to balance off the corresponding line, no one has yet found a formula to indicate meter in Hebrew poetry. Thus, the half lines may correspond to each other in a synonymous, antithetical, analogical, or staircase fashion. The synonymous parallelism merely repeats the same thought in different words, while the antithetical contrasts the thought in the first half line. The analogical builds the thought by giving a "like" or "as" clause to match the first statement, and the staircase type repeats part or all of the preceding line or two in order to make a climactic statement in the third or fourth line.

The teaching in the Psalms is a most exalted theology of God and his works. Especially significant is the strong messianic emphasis. The New Testament cites fifteen psalms as being fulfilled in the birth, life, death, and resurrection of Christ. The most direct Messianic Psalms are 2, 22, 24, 45, 72, 89, 110, 118. The names attributed to the coming Christ in the Psalms are "Servant," "Priest," "Stone," "Son of Man," and "God."

Some people are troubled over the cries for vengeance in the Psalms. Eighteen psalms have an element of cursing or imprecation, and David is the author of almost all of these. Yet he, of all people, was the least vindictive person, for when he had the chance to retaliate against Saul he purposely refused to do so. Therefore, these prayers are not cries for personal vengeance, but cries to God to vindicate his name and to preserve the office and the mission of his plan of salvation against those who have tried to usurp the cause of God and Christ in the world. David rightly viewed these attacks as assaults on the line, office, and program of the Messiah who was to come. That is why he called out to God for such drastic action—action that he personally refused to take or to urge in his own behalf.

The Psalms provide a great study for all who will take the time to explore their riches. May your heart be uplifted to God in praise of his holy name and may your prayer life be strengthened by the expressions of adoration and petition found in this sacred songbook of Israel and now of the church. May these studies bring you heart to heart with God.

Study 1
Listen and Learn

Psalms 1 and 19

Imagine that you are hiking in a remote mountainous region. The sun begins setting before you reach your destination, and the light of day is fading fast! Night falls, and you can barely see the path in front of you. Fortunately, you are traveling with a seasoned hiker who knows the twists and turns of these treacherous trails better than anyone else. As you inch your way through the darkness you listen for each word of instruction from your fellow hiker. As you listen to his confident voice, you finally reach your destination. With a sigh of relief you realize you could never have made this journey on your own.

Life can often feel like a faith-walk through dark and shadowy valleys. We need a voice to guide us on the slippery trails and uneven paths of life. The book of Psalms has helped God's people find their way through the darkness for thousands of years. These words of instruction and guidance continue to shed light on the paths of believers.

As we begin our study of Psalms, we naturally ask, "Where does one begin when there are 150 psalms to choose from?" With such a beautiful variety of psalms such as songs of praise, heartfelt prayers, sorrowful complaints, historical remembrances, and worship liturgies, where should we begin?

Why not start at the beginning: Psalm 1? After all, it was intended to introduce the Psalter. Just as important, Psalm 1 is one of the so-called Torah Psalms. *Torah* means "instruction" or "direction." These are the kind of psalms that give us the direction we need on the dark paths of life. This heading emphasizes the idea that the psalms were meant to instruct and to teach God's people, to give light in the darkness, to guide us along the path. All this we will discover as we allow the Holy Spirit to illuminate our way with the light of his Word.

1. Describe a time when you had to walk or move about in darkness, as on a camping trip or during a power blackout. What were the dangers you faced?

   What was one time you experienced darkness in your life and God's word gave you instruction and light?

2. Read Psalm 1. If some psalms are intended to instruct us, why do some believers use the Psalms only as a means of praise?

   How have you experienced the instructive function of the Psalms in either a private or corporate worship setting?

3. What do you think it means to

   — *Walk* in the counsel of the wicked?

   — *Stand* in the way of sinners?

   — *Sit* in the seat of mockers?

What is the significance of this progression of walking, standing, and sitting?

4. According to Psalm 1:2, in what aspect of a person's life is the battle for control really decided?

5. Compare the image of believers growing like a tree in Psalm 1:3–5 to the image of a tree in Jeremiah 17:5–8. Which passage is more explicit about the judgment that awaits the wicked?

   Describe what the figures and images really mean.

6. Read Psalm 19. What impact can the silent language of God's glorious creation have on a nonbeliever's knowledge of Christ (vv. 1–6)?

7. The word *perfect* in verse 7 means "all-encompassing"—like the circuit of the sun (v. 6). What is the psalmist claiming for the instruction of God?

How have you experienced the truth of this claim in your spiritual life?

8. How can the study of God's word do the following things (vv. 7–8)?

   — Revive us

   — Make us wise

   — Give us joy

   — Bring us light

9. "Words" in verse 14 repeats the same concept rendered "speech" in verses 2–3. How do these verses express the all-encompassing nature of the instruction of God for all people?

10. How can you grow more attentive to God's voice speaking through creation?

11. How can you more faithfully learn and follow the teaching of God's truth revealed in Scripture?

What will help you speak words that reflect the Word of God and please the Lord?

But his delight is in the law of the LORD, and on his law he meditates day and night.

—Psalm 1:2

Between Studies

Take time to meditate on the instruction that comes from the powerful declaration of God's presence in the heavens and the earth as well as the words he has given to us in Scripture.

STUDY 2
GOD IS KING

PSALM 2

Sometimes in songs of praise we use terms like "King of kings" and "Lord of lords" to describe God. These titles of honor reflect our allegiance and commitment. They have a ring of sovereignty, majesty, and royalty—and well they should! Our God rules over all. He is the mighty maker of heaven and earth. Our God is King!

Psalm 2 is part of a group of psalms known as "The Royal Psalms." All of these speak of kingship and the reign of God's Sovereign Son. Psalm 2 is usually seen as a coronation Psalm that describes the coming rule of the Christ. This rule is cosmic in scope; Christ will reign over the entire earth and, indeed, the entire universe.

This Psalm gives a serious warning to all the nations of the earth. God wants them to change their ways immediately and start serving and worshiping the Son lest they be destroyed.

Psalm 2 presents us with this very real issue: Who really rules the world? Is it the rulers and leaders of the people? Or is it the Lord and his Son? For Psalm 2 the answer is abundantly clear: The Lord Messiah reigns!

1. What images come to mind when you think of a king or a queen?

What do you perceive as the role of these earthly rulers?

2. If you were the sovereign ruler of your country, what would you do?

   What are some possible consequences when an evil or wicked person becomes a ruler?

3. Read Psalm 2. In what ways are some present-day religious, philosophical, and political theories aimed at breaking God's hold over all things?

4. The Hebrew word for "plot" in Psalm 2:1 is the same word translated "meditate" in Psalm 1:2. What are some other similarities and comparisons you find in Psalms 1 and 2?

5. What is so amusing to God about the nations' turmoil and plots against him and his Anointed One in verse 4?

   Identify some things we individuals or our nation does that might make God laugh.

6. The centerpiece of the whole psalm comes in verses 6–7. Many people believe this declaration was a continuation of the promises made in 2 Samuel 7:13–19. How far-reaching was this declaration?

What did this declaration include, according to this passage?

7. On what day specifically was the "today" of verse 7 fulfilled, according to Paul's famous speech in Acts 13:33?

In what sense did the resurrection of Jesus from the grave mark the beginning of a new age and the beginning of eternity (see Hebrews 6:5)?

8. What significance do you see in the fact that the book of Revelation quotes verse 9 of this psalm three times: once concerning the victorious believer (Revelation 2:27) and twice concerning the Messiah (12:5; 19:15)?

In what sense will we rule and reign with Christ *now* and in the *future?*

21

9. In verses 10–12, what prophetic advice does the psalmist give to the kings and rulers of this earth as a warning?

In what ways must this same message be given to the present-day leaders of our nation?

10. How can we help our nation to grow in deeper submission to God and his Son Jesus Christ?

11. How can we submit our lives to the lordship of God and his only Son?

How can we worship and honor God as our King, Sovereign, and Ruler?

Memory Verse
"I will proclaim the decree of the LORD: He said to me, 'You are my Son; today I have become your Father.'"

—Psalm 2:7

Take time to meditate on the royal splendor and awesome majesty of the King of kings. Praise God for his sovereign rule over your life, and pray for him to rule over the affairs of your country and the whole world. If there are specific national or world affairs that appear to be corrupted by the evil work of people, pray for God's reign to move powerfully into those circumstances.

PRAISING GOD'S MAJESTY

PSALMS 117 AND 100

The last words in the book of Psalms are this jubilant shout: "Let everything that has breath praise the LORD. Hallelujah." This declaration defines the whole tone and theme of the Psalter. Many of the Psalms are centered on the importance of praising the majesty of God. Indeed, the very title of the book means the playing of a stringed instrument. From this concept came the extended meaning of a song, usually with the background idea of stringed instrumental accompaniment to the singing.

Therefore, the Psalms are music without notes. Many of these songs focus on praising God's majesty. Some contend that "Prayers" might be a more appropriate title for the Psalter. But we notice immediately that the real burden of the prayers in the Psalms is their total absorption with who God is and what he has done. Invariably these thoughts, no matter how deep the pain that led the psalmist to pray, quickly led to shouts of praise and thanksgiving for who God is and what he had done or was going to do.

The praise psalms fall into two categories: *descriptive* praise and *declarative* praise. In the former group, the psalmist lauds God's person, his qualities, and the magnificence of his name. Briefly stated, they describe the God they praise. The second group tends to focus on what God has done for his people. These psalms declare the praise of God.

1. What is one of your favorite songs of praise, and why do you enjoy it so much?

2. Read Psalm 117. According to this psalm, simply to breathe obligates us to praise God, because the goal of every living being is to praise God and to enjoy him forever. Given that praising adds nothing to the person being praised, why is it so necessary for us to offer praise?

   How does an attitude of praise affect our outlook on life?

3. God gave breath to every living being (Genesis 2:7) and wants that breath to extol him. What effects have you observed in individuals and nations that reject or ignore this invitation to praise God?

4. The two basic reasons given in Psalm 117:2 for praising God are his love and his faithfulness. These words were first given to God's people in Exodus 34:5–6. In light of the tragic events of Exodus 32–34, how can we praise God in times of struggle and pain?

5. Read Psalm 100. The invitation of this psalm is to enter the Lord's house with joy, gladness, and singing. Reflect on what has been your general attitude, expectation, and thoughts as you have gone to church week after week?

    Describe your best and your worst moments as a church attender.

6. Verse 3 makes a series of exhortations that all creatures on earth should know. What does it mean to

    — Know that the Lord is God

    — Know that he made us

    — Know that we are his people and the sheep of his pasture

    To what degree has our modern culture explicitly denied and attacked all three propositions? Explain.

7. Note the sequence of personal pronouns in verse 3. In the Hebrew, the order is *he … he … us … we … his … his.*

    What does this sequence suggest about the modern quest for self-realization, self-identity, and self-fulfillment?

How is true self-discovery dependent on having God "before" us and "behind" us?

8. What is the difference between giving thanks to God and praising his name (v. 4)?

What is one thing you are thankful for?

What is one thing you praise God for today?

9. Verse 5 gives five reasons for praising the majesty of God. How have you experienced the truth of these words?

— "The LORD is good"

— "His love endures forever"

— "His faithfulness continues through all generations"

Memory Verse Know that the LORD is God. It is he who made us, and we are his; we are his people, the sheep of his pasture.

—Psalm 100:3

The Westminster Shorter Catechism asks in its first question: "What is the chief end of [humanity]?" The answer it gives is the one we should all echo with praise in our hearts: "[Humanity's] chief end is to glorify God and enjoy him forever."

Take time to memorize and to meditate on this question and answer.

STUDY 4

HOW GREAT IS OUR GOD?

PSALM 139

Psalm 139 answers the question, "How great is our God?" as completely as any other passage of Scripture. In this psalm we learn that our God knows everything (He is omniscient), he is everywhere (He is omnipresent), and he can do all things (He is omnipotent). Our minds can only begin to comprehend an infinitely small portion of God's greatness.

While the focus of this psalm is on the Lord himself, these attributes are applied in a way that reveals who our Lord is in relationship to his people. He knows us better than we know ourselves. His presence permeates all of creation, and there is no place, even in the highest heavens, that he does not invade. His powers are beyond human understanding and description.

Verses 17 and 18, in particular, offer great words of reassurance. The psalmist reminds us that trying to number all the thoughts about who God is and what he has done is like trying to count the grains of sand on a beach. The task is just too enormous and beyond any imagination. Nevertheless, such immensity and incomparability of being did not prevent God from being present with the psalmist. In the same way, the great Creator of heaven and earth, the Almighty God of all things, is present with us and longs for our fellowship.

1. How have you seen or experienced God's greatness in the following ways:

— In nature?

31

— In your own life?

— In the life of someone you know?

2. Read Psalm 139:1–12. How much does God know about you?

    Is that thought comforting or frightening to you? Explain your answer.

    If we truly believe God knows *everything* about us, how should this knowledge affect our lives (vv. 1–6)?

3. How would you define God's omniscience?

    If God is omniscient, why do we sometimes try to hide our actions or deeds from him?

4. What do we mean when we say God is omnipresent?

    How can this concept help and comfort hurting and lonely people?

5. What might prompt a person to want to flee from God and escape his presence?

   Identify some people in the Bible who tried to hide from God.

6. Read Psalm 139:13–24. How would you define God's omnipotence?

   Are there things God cannot do or chooses not to do? Explain your answer.

7. According to verses 13–16, when did God first establish a relationship with each of us?

   What significance does this have for the unborn?

8. What do these verses suggest to us in regard to the modern search for self-worth, self-identity, and self-esteem?

9. If God knows us inside and out, it would seem advisable to open ourselves up to the divine inspection of verses 23–24. As believers today, what changes do you think God would like us to make

— In our churches?

— In our homes?

— In our country?

— In our personal lives?

Between Studies

Take time to meditate on the following attributes of God: his holiness, justice, grace, and love.

Also meditate on the three attributes discussed in this lesson: omniscience, omnipresence, and omnipotence.

WORSHIPING THE HOLY KING OF GLORY

PSALM 24

Most Bible scholars agree that the story behind Psalm 24 is found in 1 Samuel 4. This passage of Scripture recalls a time when Israel was soundly defeated by the Philistine army and lost 4,000 soldiers. In response, Israel, to use modern parlance, played the ace they had hidden up their sleeve: They brought out the ark of God. When the holy ark had appeared in battle previously under Moses' and Joshua's leadership, the nation had proved invincible.

The ark was brought from the tabernacle in Shiloh, and a mighty shout went up from the men of Israel as it entered the camp. Their shouts of joy quickly turned to cries of defeat. Even with the ark of God before them, Israel lost 30,000 troops in their next battle. To make matters worse, the priest Eli's two sons, Hophni and Phinehas, were killed; the ark, the symbol of the presence and holiness of God, was captured and taken to the land of the Philistines. When Eli heard the battle report, he fell over backward, broke his neck, and died. Phinehas's wife went into labor, bore a son, and named him "Ichabod" as she was dying. The boy's symbolic name said it all: "The glory [of God] has departed."

Why had this happened? Why didn't the ark "work" for them as it had in Israel's glorious past? Israel had treated the ark of God as if it were a magic box. They had forgotten that it represented the holiness of God's presence in their midst.

The Philistines soon learned that they had more than they could handle. Every place where the ark of God went in their nation, that city was afflicted with rats and the bubonic plague.

Therefore, they arranged an experiment to see whether this outbreak of pestilence was just a coincidence or was from the God of the Hebrews. The Philistines made a new cart, hitched it to two cows that had just given birth, placed the ark on it, and then watched to see if the cows would carry the ark unescorted back to the land of the Hebrews. They did!

As the ark came into Israel, curious Hebrews gathered around and gawked at it. Immediately, seventy men died. This led to the agonizing question: "Who can stand in the presence of the LORD, this holy God?"

God cannot be manipulated; he cannot be compromised; he cannot be trivialized. He is the holy God who reigns over all. Who can stand in the presence of the holy God? Only those with "clean hands and a pure heart."

1. What images come to your mind when you think of the holiness of God?

    What in our lives can lead to personal holiness?

    What things can lead a person away from holiness?

2. Read Psalm 24. When we prepare to worship God, what does it mean in practical terms to

    — Be people of clean hands

    — Be people of clean hearts

    — Keep from lifting our souls to idols

    — Refrain from swearing by what is false

3. Verses 1–2 say that the Lord owns the earth and everything in it. Read Psalm 96:10 and note that two words, "world" and "established," appear in both psalms. How does that add to your appreciation of Psalm 24?

4. Preparation for worshiping God is both external and internal: "hands" and "heart" (v. 4). What are some illustrations of preparation for worship from the history of Israel and from your own personal experience? Be sure to consider both internal and external preparations.

5. Verses 4–5 bring to mind the principal concerns for biblical morality. These and other principles are listed in Psalm 15. On the basis of these two psalms, name the basic characteristics that describe the person who would come to God's house and worship the Lord.

—
—
—
—
—
—
—

How can we develop these qualities in our lives?

6. Verse 5 gives us a promise of "blessing" and "vindication" from God. What does this verse have in common with the promise of blessing found in the Beatitudes (Matthew 5:3–12)?

7. God told Moses that no one could see his face and live (Exodus 33:17–23). If this is true, what does the psalmist mean in Psalm 24:6?

   What can we do to grow in our seeking the Lord's face?

8. Read Matthew 21:4–9. How is this passage a fulfillment of Psalm 24:7–10?

9. Christ was not crowned "King of Glory" at his first advent. According to Revelation 19:11–16, what may be expected when he comes the second time?

   How will the words of Psalm 24:7–10 be realized by Christ's actions in that day?

10. How should we worship the King of Glory as we await his
    triumphant return?

Memory   Who may ascend the hill of the LORD?
Verse   Who may stand in his holy place?
         He who has clean hands and a pure heart,
         who does not lift up his soul to an idol
         or swear by what is false.

         —Psalm 24:3–4

Between Studies

Take time to praise God for ruling over the entire universe as the
Mighty King. Begin by thinking of the small details of your life and
acknowledge his rule over them. Reflect on your church and community, and pray for his gracious rule to increase in these places.
Think next about your state, your country, and the whole world, and
praise the Lord for his kingship over all of these things. Finally, let
your mind wander to the farthest reaches of time and space and
acknowledge the sovereign rule of the Lord as King over all things.

It might be helpful to do this reflection in a journal and to write
out your praises.

STUDY 6
PRAYING OUT OF THE DEPTHS OF OUR SINFULNESS

PSALM 130

"Out of the depths." That is where this psalm comes from. In pain, loneliness, fear, sinfulness, and uncertainty the psalmist cries out to the Lord.

Have you ever felt so low that you sensed your prayers were being lifted from the pit of despair and pain? If so, you will be able to identify with the heartbeat of this psalm. It reflects the importance of honest confession and seeking out the Lord in the midst of our struggles, sin, and pain.

Martin Luther found in this psalm an expression of the unmerited grace and forgiveness of God that reflects the heart of the Gospel. One of Luther's best-known hymns is a version of this psalm. Another reformer, Theodore Beza, was said to have died with the words of this psalm on his lips. It is also said that St. Augustine inscribed the words of this psalm, among others, on the walls of his bedroom during his final illness so that he could meditate on the words.

Further, on the afternoon when John Wesley found his heart "strangely warmed" at a room at Aldersgate, he heard the words of Psalm 130 sung as an anthem at St. Paul's cathedral.

This psalm is a mirror of the human plight, but it is also a window that opens onto God's gracious forgiveness and restoration. Just as

41

this psalm has been a point of spiritual growth for believers through the centuries, it can challenge us today.

1. Recall a time when you experienced pain and struggle and found yourself crying out to the Lord. How did you experience the Lord's presence and comfort during this time?

2. Read Psalm 130. Why is it often difficult for people to offer forgiveness to one another?

   Why do we sometimes wait until we are "in the pits" before we ask God to forgive us?

3. The "depths" from which the psalmist cries brings to mind the picture of a shipwrecked sailor calling out from the turbulent waters of the sea as he fights for each breath of life. What are some other pictures of the threats and "depths" that people face that could cause them to cry out to the Lord as the psalmist does?

4. Why is it significant that the psalmist can still be heard by God even though he calls to him during a raging storm?

   Identify some other occasions in the Bible when distress signals from God's people have been the motivating factor for his bringing rescue and deliverance.

5. Why does the psalmist say what he does in verse 3?

   What does he imply about God's knowledge and response to our sin?

6. Three affirmations of hope are offered in this psalm. What does each mean?

   — God offers forgiveness (v. 4)

   — God offers steadfast love (grace) (v. 7)

   — God offers full redemption (v. 7)

7. If the way out of the depths is through God's forgiveness, what part do hope and anticipation play (vv. 5–8)?

8. What does it mean to "wait" or "hope" in the Lord?

   Who or what is the object of our hope and confidence for the future?

How does our view of hope compare with where our generation has placed its confidence and hope for the future?

9. Verses 7–8 indicate that our experience of God is not exhausted and does not totally end with our individual deliverance from forgiveness: there is more. What else happens beyond our experience of forgiveness?

10. Some people pray to God as if his phone number were only 911, for use only in emergencies. What are other proper functions and circumstances for prayer?

Memory Verse
I wait for the LORD, my soul waits, and in his word I put my hope.

—Psalm 130: 5

Between Studies

God will forgive all who call upon him in spite of the enormity of the crime or the circumstances. Take time today to confess your sins honestly to the Lord and seek his forgiveness. Ask God to help you know his grace and also to walk in hope even during the storms of life.

STUDY 7
CONFESSING OUR TRANSGRESSIONS
PSALMS 51 AND 32

The story of the day King David strolled onto the upper floor of his palace and saw a beautiful woman bathing, setting into motion a tragic series of events, is legendary.

David found out that the woman was Bathsheba, the wife of Uriah the Hittite—one of David's own soldiers, currently on the battlefield in defense of the empire. Unwisely, David sent for her and slept with her, and she became pregnant. To cover up his sin, David sent for her husband and encouraged him to return home to "enjoy" his wife. David's hope was that Uriah would sleep with his wife and later believe the child was his own.

Amazingly, Uriah steadfastly refused to indulge in physical pleasure and sleep with his wife while his comrades were still risking their lives on the battlefield. Yet David had avoided going to battle and had wantonly indulged his physical desires. Quite a contrast!

In desperation David ordered Uriah be placed in the forefront of the battle and left unprotected as the rest of the troops suddenly pulled back from the battle. The ploy worked, and Uriah was killed.

By this time David was guilty of breaking half of the Ten Commandments. He had coveted, killed, committed adultery, stolen another man's wife, and had borne false witness. But all of this had not left David unscarred. Psalm 32 describes how David felt after his sin and before his confession. He decided to keep quiet about it and to "tough" it out, as they say. But it seemed as if his strength was disappearing and his bones were going to crumble. Finally, he concluded,

"I will confess my transgression to the LORD" (Psalm 32:5). Oh, what a relief! Psalm 51 is the record of David's confession before the Lord.

1. Why do you think history repeats itself so often?

    How has there been a tragic repeating of history in the following areas:

    — In the church?

    — In families?

    — In our nation?

2. Read Psalm 51. Why did David appeal to the character of God at the beginning of his prayer of confession (v. 1)?

    What three attributes of God did David rely on as he confessed his sins?

3. Read Psalm 32. In verses 3–4 David refused to acknowledge his sin. What are some of the potential consequences when we hold onto our sin and refuse to confess and repent?

    — Physically

    — Emotionally

    — Spiritually

4. When David regained his senses about this whole affair, he came to three conclusions. What did he conclude about

    — God's attitude toward his sin (Psalm 51:4)?

    — Himself and his actions (Psalm 32:5)?

    — His own nature as a human being (Psalm 51:5)?

    To what degree are these same factors true of all people as sinners?

5. David restated the plea he made in Psalm 51:1–2 in verses 7–15 with a series of appeals. He asked God to "cleanse," "wash," and "renew" him. Where, according to verses 6 and 10, does God desire the work of cleansing to begin, and why?

    What can we do to seek this cleansing?

6. Why do you think verse 16 says that God does not delight in sacrifices, yet verse 19 declares that "then there will be righteous sacrifices"?

7. The word *create* in verse 10 paints a vivid picture of God doing something new. What was David asking God to do that was brand new?

8. What promise did David make to the Lord in verse 13?

   How can we follow his example and help other sinners discover God's grace and return to the Lord?

   How does this verse reflect the spirit of Matthew 28:20?

9. How does the analogy of a bit in the mouth of a horse relate to God's teaching, instruction, and guidance (Psalm 32:8–9)?

10. Why is forgiveness of our sins essential if we are to find guidance and understand the will of God for our lives?

Memory
Verse
The sacrifices of God are a broken spirit;
a broken and contrite heart,
O God, you will not despise.

—Psalm 51:17

Only through the wonderful and free forgiveness of God can we be prepared to enter God's presence and be assured of his guidance in our lives. Take time to praise the Lord for opening the door to forgiveness through the sacrificial death of his Son, Jesus Christ. Also, pray for opportunities to declare God's love and to help others turn from sin and receive the grace of God in Jesus.

THE LORD IS PRESENT

PSALMS 23 AND 46

I t is safe to say that Psalm 23 is the best-known passage in the entire Old Testament. It is rare to attend a funeral service where this beloved text is not read. The tender and soothing message of Psalm 23 offers some of the best comfort we can give to a grieving family at the loss of a loved one.

Even though most people rarely see a shepherd tending sheep, Psalm 23 continues to minister the power and grace of God. We seem to have an inner sense of the tenderness and care that a shepherd gives to his sheep. This image makes sense to us as we think about the gentle and protective love the Lord has for all of his children, the sheep of his pasture.

Psalms 23 and 46 emphasize this assurance by affirming the presence of God. In these psalms we learn that our God is the one who is always "with us." In fact, this is one of the names given to our Lord Jesus Christ: Immanuel, "God with us."

Psalm 23:4 has at the heart of its message the assurance that "You are with me." Psalm 46:7 gives this same comforting affirmation: "The LORD Almighty is with us." Both psalms offer great hope and strength as we follow the Lord along life's highway.

1. Recall a time when you clearly experienced the comfort and care of your heavenly shepherd.

2. Read Psalm 23. In a culture that "wants everything" and wishes to "lack nothing," how can we declare, "The LORD is my shepherd, I shall lack [or want] nothing"?

    According to verse 1, who or what is the only necessity of life?

    How does this teaching relate to Matthew 6:25, 33?

3. Verses 2–3 do not mean that God promises to give us a life of complete peace and constant tranquillity. What do they mean?

    How does the image of grazing sheep help us understand the meaning?

4. Why should the "the valley of the shadow of death" bring no fear to God's people?

    The "rod" and "staff" are symbols of God's rule, authority, and guidance. How do the spiritual rod and staff of the Lord bring us comfort?

5. The image in verses 5–6 has God inviting us into his house as an honored guest. There he promises his constant "goodness" and "love." How do we experience God's love?

How do we experience God's goodness?

6. Read Psalm 46. This psalm paints a picture of cosmic turmoil. In verses 2–3 we see the equivalent of an earthquake that measures about 9.8 on the Richter Scale, a hurricane of class 5 magnitude, and a tidal wave 100 feet high. What does the psalmist say we can trust when the whole world seems to be coming apart?

7. What does it mean to "be still, and know that I am God" (v. 10)?

8. What are some things in life that make it hard to "be still"?

What can we do to help us slow down and in tranquillity discover the presence of God?

9. On the basis of verses 8–9, how can God make "smart bombs," Patriot missiles, and nuclear warheads—the weapons of war—cease to exist?

    Where else in the Scriptures does God promise to do this?

10. This psalm begins and ends with the affirmation that God is our "fortress." What do the following statements mean to you?

    — God is my refuge

    — God is my strength

    — God is my help

Memory Verse   "Be still and know that I am God;
I will be exalted among the nations,
I will be exalted in the earth."

—Psalm 46:10

Between Studies

Take time in the coming week to pray for people you know who are going through difficult times and need to experience the tender comfort and care of the Lord. Also, take time to call someone you know who has lost a loved one in the past year or two. Allow the Lord to use you as a vehicle of his comfort and compassion.

STUDY 9
ON THE EDGE
OF UNBELIEF

PSALM 73

ave you ever been so aware of the evil and injustice in the world that you just wanted to scream, "Why? Why, Lord?" Maybe you were watching the news on television and were overwhelmed by endless parade of human tragedy, pain, and suffering. Maybe you received news of a great injustice: another drunk driver has walked away from an accident where innocent people were killed, another husband has abandoned his wife and children to seek personal pleasure, another criminal has been set free because of a legal technicality—and the list goes on. "Why?" we ask.

If you have ever felt like this, Psalm 73 will be of great comfort to you. The psalmist's confidence and self-assurance were destroyed. His faith was about to slip over the edge of a slippery slope into unbelief. We can understand his inner turmoil: he was unable to explain why the wicked are so prosperous. "Why?" he asks.

This psalm takes a sudden turn in verse 17, however, when the psalmist goes into the sanctuary of God and thinks about the final end of the wicked. By the end of the psalm, a calmer perspective is restored. The main focus of Psalm 73 is that God still reigns in spite of the appearance that evil—and evil persons—has triumphed.

1. What was an occasion when you became deeply aware of the evil and injustice in this world?

Why do experiences like these sometimes challenge our faith?

2. Read Psalm 73:1–20. Some people preach and believe the "health and wealth gospel"—the idea that the Bible teaches that good health and material prosperity are guaranteed to all who believe in Jesus. What is wrong with this message?

3. How can the psalmist state that God is "good" to all who are "pure in heart" (v. 1) and then tell how he almost lost his faith at seeing the wicked prosper?

   Why are these two seemingly contradictory statements actually compatible?

4. Verses 4–9 and 12 describe the state of the wicked. What do they say about

   — The state of the wicked?

   — The experiences of the wicked?

   — The health of the wicked?

   — The attitudes of the wicked?

Is this an accurate a picture of the wicked in today's world? Explain your answer.

5. What effect do the wicked have on the faithful (vv. 10–11)?

What effect does the prosperity of the wicked have on the psalmist (vv. 13–14)?

Why might we sometimes have the attitude of the psalmist expresses in verse 13?

6. At first the psalmist sees himself on slippery and uncertain ground (vv. 2–3). Later the situation changes: the wicked are now on the slippery slope (vv. 18–20). What happened to reverse the thinking and perception of the psalmist?

7. Read Psalm 73:21–28. Finally the psalmist comes to his senses and sees things as the Lord sees them. How does he regard his behavior before his attitude changed (vv. 21–22)?

In what ways do we sometimes act and think as the psalmist did?

8. How do you think God responds to people who doubt him?

When might our doubt be justified?

When are doubting and questioning God dangerous?

9. What hope does the psalmist express in verses 24–25?

How does this hope still give believers strength even when affairs of life don't seem to line up with God's will and ways?

Memory Verse
You guide me with your counsel,
and afterward you will take me into glory.
Whom have I in heaven but you?
And earth has nothing I desire besides you.

—Psalm 73: 24–25

Between Studies

This psalm has been the favorite psalm of many. Charles Wesley found it his final consolation as he was on his deathbed. After writing 6,500 hymns, his final song was based in part on Psalm 73:25: "Whom have I in heaven but you? And being with you, I desire nothing on earth."

Reflect on the things in your life that bring anxiety. Lay these before the Lord and ask him to help you cast all your burdens on him.

(If you have a psaltery hymnal, look up Wesley's hymn or another version of Psalm 73 and meditate on it.)

COMING TO TERMS WITH TIME

PSALM 90

This psalm is about time—God's time and ours. It is interesting to note that Moses, a man who ran out of time, wrote this psalm. In fact, this is the only psalm attributed to him.

After Moses had led Israel through the wilderness for forty years, God denied his request to take the nation of Israel into the Promised Land. God's reason is that he was angry with Moses. In Numbers 20:10 Moses had stolen glory from God when he implied that he and Aaron could bring water out of the rock by force instead of simply speaking to the rock as God had instructed. The Lord wanted the people to know their needs would be met by his word alone.

Moses changed the focus from God to himself by saying, "Listen, you rebels, must *we* bring you water out of this rock?"

Who had said anything about Moses and Aaron's ability to do such a great miracle? Thus Moses stole the credit and glory from God. God wanted to teach his people that their belief in his word was more important than their parched throats.

So God barred Moses from the Promised Land. The clock ticked on, and the people remained in the wilderness. Before the time came to enter the land, Moses was dead.

1. How would you answer the charge that God appears to be arbitrary or unpredictable or unfair in cutting some people's lives short and in letting others live to a very old age?

2. Read Psalm 90:1–12. Moses uses two verbs in verse 2 that are usually reserved for speaking of childbirth. What are these verbs, and what do they express?

What does this verse teach us about the God we worship?

3. Verse 3 emphasizes human mortality. How is this verse related to Genesis 3:19?

What do you think is God's purpose in reminding us of this condition?

4. What is the difference between God's perception of time and our perception of time?

What aspects of God's character are being stressed in this psalm?

5. What is it in human beings that provokes God to anger and wrath (vv. 7–9)?

What happened in Moses' life that made him confront God's fury? (See Number 20:1–13; Deuteronomy 1:37; 3:26.)

6. In light of the brevity of our lives, what is the psalmist asking God to "teach" us in verses 10–12?

   What can we do to obey this exhortation?

7. Read Psalm 90:13–17. In verses 13–14 God is asked to "relent," to "turn," or to "repent" (all possible translations of the same Hebrew word). Is Moses asking God to make everyone's life last longer? If not, then what is Moses asking God to do?

8. How can God change, or "relent," if Scripture teaches that he is unchanging?

9. How can we be "satisfied in the morning" and be made "glad" all our days (v. 14)?

   What deep spiritual truths bring a real joy to your life?

Why is this different from "positive thinking" or ordinary psychological counseling?

10. What makes "the work of our hands" and our time on earth meaningful, joyful, and enduring beyond our days (vv. 16–17)?

How should this understanding affect our investment of time, energy, and talents?

Memory
Verse

Teach us to number our days aright,
that we may gain a heart of wisdom.

—Psalm 90:12

Between Studies

Take time to evaluate your life and use of time. Look at your schedule for the past week and the coming week and consider ways in which you have used time wisely or unwisely. Ask the Lord to help you use your time for matters that are pleasing to him.

STUDY 11
STANDING BENEATH
THE CROSS OF JESUS

PSALM 22

salm 22 has sometimes been called "the fifth gospel" because it so graphically predicts and depicts the suffering, death, and resurrection of Christ. It is the most frequently quoted Psalm in the Passion narratives of the four Gospels.

From the beginning to the end of Jesus' ordeal on the cross, this psalm was the one that refreshed his soul. Two of the Gospel writers record that he cried out, "My God, my God, why have you forsaken me?" (Matthew 27:46; Mark 15:34). These words come directly from the first verse of this psalm.

Jesus also cried, "It is finished" (John 19:30). This is a translation of a word that comes from the very last verse of this psalm. It appears that all of Psalm 22 went through the heart and mind of the Savior as he hung on the cross.

Moreover, those in the crowd who mocked Jesus there unwittingly gave fulfillment to the words of Psalm 22:7–8: "He trusts in the LORD; let the LORD rescue him, since he delights in him" (see Matthew 27:39–43; Mark 15:29). Jesus' thirst in John 19:28 fulfilled the word predicted in Psalm 22:15. Even the division of Jesus' garments and the soldiers' gambling for his robe were anticipated in Psalm 22:18 (see Matthew 27:35; Mark 15:24; Luke 23:34; John 19:23–24). The connections between this psalm and the Passion accounts found in the Gospels are startling.

1. What mental pictures do you see when you think of the suffering and crucifixion of Jesus?

    Although remembering the death of Jesus can be painful, why is it important for us to never forget what he suffered?

2. Read Psalm 22:1–21. How would you describe the feelings of the psalmist in verses 1–2?

    Describe the emotions of believers who pray and cry out to God and feel that their prayers are not heard.

3. Verse 3 can be translated "Yet you are holy, enthroned on the praises of Israel." This means that God's presence dwells not only in the Holy of Holies, but also in the hearts and praises of his people. What implications does this have regarding the choruses and hymns we sing in praise of God?

    What is a hymn or praise chorus that you believe gives glory to God?

4. How many parallels relating to the onlooking crowd can you find between these verses and the Gospel accounts of Jesus' crucifixion?

5. Of what significance is it that the sufferer's mother is mentioned in this psalm, but not his father (vv. 9–10)?

6. What three things does the sufferer pray for in verses 19–21?

   How would you respond to the charge that the Father failed to answer this prayer when Christ suffered on the cross?

7. Read Psalm 22:22–31. How does the tone and focus of the psalm shift at verse 22?

   How does this section of the psalm answer the cry for help spoken in verse 1?

8. What is the scope or range of thanksgiving to God in this psalm (vv. 27–31)?

How can a person have thanksgiving in the midst of suffering?

9. On three different occasions God speaks of his work as being finished or completed. What is the significance of each?

— On the seventh day of creation (Genesis 1:31)

— On the cross (John 19:30)

— At the end of history (Revelation 21:6)

How does each event act as a divider between the great eras of God's work?

Memory Verse

All the ends of the earth
will remember and turn to the LORD,
and all the families of the nations
will bow down before him,
for dominion belongs to the LORD
and he rules over the nations.

—Psalm 22:27–28

Between Studies

Take time to read the accounts of Christ's suffering and death in the Gospels. Praise Jesus for giving himself as the payment for your sins. Also, ask God to give you strength to hold onto his hand as you go through times of suffering. He has walked this road, and he can help you through your trials and pain.

STUDY 12
WALKING AROUND ZION

PSALMS 48 AND 122

O ne of the great delights in visiting Jerusalem is to take a walking tour around the city on top of her walls. It is a spectacular sight. Much has been written about how Jerusalem has been the center of struggles between people and nations for thousands of years. The city has been sacked and destroyed some seventeen times. The site of Jerusalem, often called "Zion, city of God," is about as central to the program of God in the past, present, and future as Jesus of Nazareth is to the story of the Gospels and the message of Christianity.

Yet the city stands also as God's metaphor and symbol that God cares for his people. In Psalms 48 and 122 Jerusalem serves as a symbol of God's intimate presence with and protection of his people. Jerusalem is "the city of the Great King" (Psalm 48:2) and the site of the temple, "the house of the LORD" (Psalm 122:1).

Psalm 122 belongs to a collection of fifteen psalms that are called Psalms of Ascent, because they were presumably written as a short songbook for the pilgrims to use as they went up to Jerusalem to the three annual feasts celebrated there. Both Psalm 48 and 122 belong to the group of psalms known as the Songs of Zion. All the psalms in this group focus on Jerusalem as Zion, "the city of the LORD Almighty."

Because Jerusalem symbolizes the presence of God, "walking around Zion" can mean more than looking down on a beautiful city and temple mount. It means that we have an intimate relationship with our God and Savior.

1. Recall a place where you sensed the presence of God in a special way. What made the place and the occasion memorable?

2. Read Psalm 48:1–8. What makes Jerusalem beautiful in the eyes of the pilgrim-psalmist (vv. 1–3)?

3. The imposing walls of the city upon the hilltop were designed to help protect Jerusalem from its enemies. What are some of the attacks and events the psalmist might have in mind in verses 4–8?

    In what sense was the city's safety dependent on God rather than on walls?

4. Read Psalm 48:9–14. God's "praise" and his "right hand" are mentioned in verse 10. What are the contrasting characteristics of God suggested in these two terms?

    What are some of the effects of meditating on God's unfailing love, righteousness, and judgments?

5. Note the five imperative verbs in verses 12–14. Why is it important to tell the next generation about God's unfailing love?

6. Read Psalm 122. Imagine that you are a pilgrim visiting Jerusalem for the first time. What are the "first impressions" of the psalmist as expressed in verses 1–4?

7. What themes and ideas do you find in common between this psalm and Psalm 48?

8. What words and thoughts in the psalm imply the unity of believers and the sense of being together?

9. In what ways is "peace" political, and in what ways is it spiritual (vv. 6–8)?

10. The first and last verses both speak of "the house of the LORD." Why is it important to be in "the house of the Lord"?

Many of us are not really glad when people say to us, "Let us go into the house of the Lord." Why do you think this is so, and what can we do to remedy this sad state of affairs?

As we have heard,
so have we seen
in the city of the LORD Almighty,
in the city of our God:
God makes her secure forever.

—Psalm 48:8

Between Studies

Think about your "brothers [and sisters] and friends" in the household of faith. Consider ways that individually and in cooperation with them you can promote the peace and unity of the church as you "walk around Zion."

LEADER'S NOTES

L eading a Bible discussion—especially for the first time—can make you feel both nervous and excited. If you are nervous, realize that you are in good company. Many biblical leaders, such as Moses, Joshua, and the apostle Paul, felt nervous and inadequate to lead others (see, for example, 1 Corinthians 2:3). Yet God's grace was sufficient for them, just as it will be for you.

Some excitement is also natural. Your leadership is a gift to the others in the group. Keep in mind, however, that other group members also share responsibility for the group. Your role is simply to stimulate discussion by asking questions and encouraging people to respond. The suggestions listed below can help you to be an effective leader.

Preparing to Lead

1. Ask God to help you understand and apply the passage to your own life. Unless that happens, you will not be prepared to lead others.

2. Carefully work through each question in the study guide. Meditate and reflect on the passage as you formulate your answers.

3. Familiarize yourself with the leader's notes for the study. These will help you understand the purpose of the study and will provide valuable information about the questions in the study.

4. Pray for the various members of the group. Ask God to use these studies to make you better disciples of Jesus Christ.

5. Before the first meeting, make sure each person has a study guide. Encourage them to prepare beforehand for each study.

Leading the Study

1. Begin the study on time. If people realize that the study begins on schedule, they will work harder to arrive on time.

2. At the beginning of your first time together, explain that these studies are designed to be discussions, not lectures. Encourage everyone to participate, but realize that some may be hesitant to speak during the first few sessions.

3. Read the introductory paragraph at the beginning of the discussion. This will orient the group to the passage being studied.

4. Read the passage aloud. You may choose to do this yourself, or you might ask for volunteers.

5. The questions in the guide are designed to be used just as they are written. If you wish, you may simply read each one aloud to the group. Or you may prefer to express them in your own words. Unnecessary rewording of the questions, however, is not recommended.

6. Don't be afraid of silence. People in the group may need time to think before responding.

7. Avoid answering your own questions. If necessary, rephrase a question until it is clearly understood. Even an eager group will quickly become passive and silent if they think the leader will do most of the talking.

8. Encourage more than one answer to each question. Ask, "What do the rest of you think?" or "Anyone else?" until several people have had a chance to respond.

9. Try to be affirming whenever possible. Let people know you appreciate their insights into the passage.

10. Never reject an answer. If it is clearly wrong, ask, "Which verse led you to that conclusion?" Or let the group handle the problem by asking them what they think about the question.

11. Avoid going off on tangents. If people wander off course, gently bring them back to the passage being considered.

12. Conclude your time together with conversational prayer. Ask God to help you apply those things that you learned in the study.

13. End on time. This will be easier if you control the pace of the discussion by not spending too much time on some questions or too little on others.

   More suggestions and help are found in the book *Leading Bible Discussions* (InterVarsity Press). Reading it would be well worth your time.

Listen and Learn
Psalms 1 and 19

Purpose   To discover the different ways God speaks to us, and to see the importance of meditating on God and his instruction rather than on ourselves.

Question 2   "Instruction" does not take place only in a classroom setting, but also in private devotions and in public worship. Although the Psalms do inspire and lead us to praise, they are also meant to give practical and sound instruction for faithful living.

Question 3   "Counsel," "way," and "seat" imply the three realms of thinking, behaving, and belonging. They may also represent the three degrees, or phases, of departing from the Lord as one first accepts the advice of the wicked, then becomes a party to their ways of living and acting, and finally adopts the attitude of scoffing at things that once he or she would have held dear and sacred.

Question 4   It is in the mind that we reject the counsel of the wicked and also receive the instruction of God. People are what they think about most; minds shape lives for good or ill. Psalm 1:2 is a deliberate echo of Joshua 1:8. The battle begins in the mind, and we must be ready to guard our minds from evil and to open them to what is good and pure.

Question 5   Notice the parallels between these two passages:

Jeremiah 17:7–8	*Psalms 1:3*
like a tree planted by the water	like a tree planted by streams of water
sends out its roots by the stream	
does not fear when heat comes	
its leaves are always green	whose leaf does not wither
has no worries in the year of drought	
never fails to bear fruit	yields its fruit in season
whatever he does prospers	

Psalm 1:4, unlike Jeremiah's description of the judgment of the wicked (Jeremiah 17:6), takes it all the way up to the final judgment. Also, while Jeremiah concentrates on what the wicked see and feel, the psalmist concentrates on what that man is: rootless, fruitless, and weightless. This image is one of threshing out the grain—

beating or trampling it to break the grain out of the husk. Then the grain is thrown up into the air for the chaff to be blown away by the wind, leaving the heavier seeds to fall to the ground.

Question 6   Many scholars have divided Psalm 19 into two psalms—verses 1–6 dealing with creation, and 7–14 dealing with the Torah, or "law." This division is unnecessary because the two themes are complementary. Furthermore, this division obscures the fact that the instruction of the Lord is built right into the very fabric and structure of the universe. The instruction found in the natural world we call "natural revelation"; the instruction found in the Word of God we call "special revelation."

Note Romans 1:18–23; 10:18. These verses declare that God's eternal power and deity are clearly revealed in the created realm of nature. They speak to everyone.

Question 7   Both the rotational movement of the sun and the breadth and depth of the instruction of God found in his Word declare that his teaching embraces everything—every aspect of life and every human endeavor.

Question 8   God's Word and revelation bring spiritual renewal of the inner person. That word will also make us wise for all kinds of situations, including, of course, making us wise to salvation (see 2 Timothy 3:15). God's instruction will also bring joy to heart and life, and it will shed light on all that we do.

Question 9   The fact that the concepts are the same in these verses is another indication that the Psalm exhibits a unity of theme. In this way the psalmist circles back to where he began as he notes that both creation and God's Word are set to instruct us. It is on this message that we must meditate and request that whatever words may be found on our lips should be pleasing and acceptable to our Lord.

Study
Two

God Is King
Psalm 2

Purpose   To show that behind all the prayers, praises, and laments in the Psalms is the answer to the question, "Who is in charge of this world?"

Question 3 The nations and kings in Psalm 2 are pictured as plotting against the Lord and his Messiah. Their desire is to throw off God's rule, control, and authority. Today the systems of relativism, pluralism, communism, the cults, and world religions all take their aim at the truth of God as it is revealed in the Bible and in Jesus Christ. They feel that if they can persuade the majority of the populace that everything is relative and without absolute truth, they will become dominant.

Question 4 Several factors suggest that Psalms 1 and 2 together form one complete introduction to the whole Psalter: (a) there is the connection between "plot" (2:1) and "meditate" (1:2); (b) Psalm 2:12 ends with the same word with which Psalm 1:1 begins: "Blessed," or "Happy"; (c) the destiny of the wicked is the same in Psalm 1:6 as in Psalm 2:12.

Psalm 1 states that the Psalter is to function as instruction from the Lord; Psalm 2 supplies the central part of that teaching—namely, the Lord and his Messiah will reign over all the world as King of kings and Lord of lords.

Question 5 The cause of divine laughter here is the sheer arrogance of these kings and rulers who feel they can do combat with God as easily as they take on one another. There is irony in the fact that these brash rulers, having been given their thrones and seats of government by the hand of God, are threatening the God that made them and allowed them to come to power.

Question 6 The installation of God's Son, the Messiah, on Zion was accompanied by the decree that God had promised to adopt one of David's heirs to be his very own son (see 2 Samuel 7:14). But in that same ancient promise made with David in 2 Samuel 7:13–19, God promised that the coming Son would have a throne, a dynasty, and a kingdom that would endure forever (v. 16). Moreover, this decree was the very means by which God would bless all the nations of the earth, just as he had promised Abraham in Genesis 12:3.

Question 7 The newly installed Messiah would formally take over his inheritance and titles on a certain day, called "today" in the Psalm. Paul vigorously argued that this day was Easter Sunday morning when Christ arose from the dead. This marked a new moment in the history of redemption, because in the resurrection Christ put all the world on notice that his rule and reign had begun and would one day arrive in full array at his second coming.

Hebrews 1:1 indicates that with the coming of Christ in his first advent, the "last days" had begun. That is why believers now have eternal life (John 3:36) and why they have been translated into the kingdom of his dear Son (Colossian 1:13) and are already enjoying a taste of the full powers they are to have when he comes again (Hebrews 6:5).

Question 8 To Christians who do God's will all the way to the end, he will grant authority over the nations (Revelation 2:26–27). That is the same status that is attributed to Christ, the male child born of the woman in Revelation 12:5. He, too, will rule over all nations with an iron scepter—and he will do this at the second coming as he leads the armies of heaven on his white horse and strikes the nations (Revelation 19:11–16).

The scepter was a symbol of government that had already been given to the tribe of Judah, through whom the Messiah would come (Genesis 49:10).

Question 9 Kings, rulers, and leaders of nations would be well-advised to "be wise." Such wisdom only begins with the "fear of the LORD." Thus, they should "observe the LORD with fear." If Psalm 1 deals with the destiny of individuals, Psalm 2 deals with the destiny of nations; but both individuals and nations have to choose between the two paths available to them. What is true on the personal level of individual piety is also true on the larger scale of world affairs, foreign policy, international alliances, and all aspirants to power on a cosmic scale.

We have seen such massive changes in world governments since Christmas 1989. All of Eastern Europe and the former Soviet Union have witnessed unprecedented changes that no one could ever have imagined even just a few years earlier. That ought to be a warning to all present-day nations to behave themselves and to honor God and his Son lest they, too, come to sudden and irreversible grief.

Study
Three

Praising God's Majesty
Psalms 117 and 100

Purpose To understand that our whole purpose in life is to praise God—that to live is to praise God and to praise God is to live.

Question 2   Praising never adds anything to the item or person being lauded; instead, praising compels our enjoyment of the object or person praised and does something for us. When we say, "That picture is beautiful," our words do not reshape, modify, or add anything to the painting; but we are enhanced as persons when we naturally and instinctively recognize what is already there. People who praise the least may become the least likable persons generally, for their souls tend to shrink to the size of their capacity to recognize and genuinely offer deserved praise to others.

Question 3   The invitation to praise God is extended to all nations and all peoples; it is not just limited to Israel. According to Psalm 150:6, everything that breathes is called on to praise the Lord because that is the goal of all creation. In Psalm 11, "all the earth" is called to praise God. But when people or nations refuse to offer praise to God, they all find their souls, outlook, and personality shrinking as they become consumed with self.

Question 4   God's grace and truth have always been the real basis for offering praise to him. We have amazingly received love and faithfulness when we have deserved nothing but his condemnation and wrath. The same truth is expressed in Exodus 34:5–6 in the account of the golden calf. Had God not been "compassionate" and "slow to anger" and "loving," Israel would have been justly destroyed for her outrageous sin.

Question 5   If the truth were known, we might find that entering God's house with joy is less common than attending for ignoble and unbiblical reasons. Too often, as children we entered God's house because we were forced to go, if we went at all. A hundred and one reasons, stated and unstated, became our primary motivator for seeking out the house of God. God wants us to renounce all these motivations and replace them with joy, gladness, and singing.

Question 6   Making any idea, person, goal, institution, or anything else equal to, or greater than, God is equivalent to questioning the declaration, "The LORD is God." Likewise, we must avoid all theories or practices that affirm we are the masters of our own fate—as if we created ourselves or we can explain how we were made apart from God. As people who belong to God, we must act like his sheep—recognizing his voice and coming to him when he calls. Our modern culture has attacked all three affirmations by raising up false gods in place of the One God.

Question 7   This arrangement of pronouns suggests that we can not find out who we are until we understand who God is, for he stands at the beginning and the end of this series with ourselves in the middle. This truth is also emphasized in Ecclesiastes 3:1; human life remains a mystery until we come to find the Lord at the beginning and end of all our existence.

Question 8   When we give thanks, we stand on the same level as the person who receives our words. But when we praise someone, we must stand on a lower level and raise the person praised to a higher pedestal and express either who they are or what they have done that has merited their being praised. Accordingly, when we come to the house of God, it must be with both an attitude of gratefulness for all that God has done and a word about how great he is.

This is not to say that there are not times when we do come with heavy hearts. But when that happens, we need to recall who God is and what he has done for us in the past so that we have hope for the immediate trial that we face.

Study Four   *How Great Is Our God?*
Psalm 139

Purpose   To reflect on the attributes of God and thereby discover a properly balanced picture of reality.

Question 2   God knows everything there is to know about us. Not one thought that passes through my mind, not one detail of my life, not one word I speak escapes his notice. Nothing is hid from his all-knowing and searching eye. This thought can be both comforting and frightening, depending on what we have said or done that we wish God did not know. Therefore, even though we cannot do it perfectly, we should seek to live a life that will pass his approval and inspection all the time and everywhere in everything.

Question 3   Because God knows the totality of my being, he is able to detect anything in my heart and mind regardless of how deeply I bury it inside (vv. 2, 4). We are open books to God that he can easily read. Therefore, omniscience is that attribute of God by which he knows everything about all persons: attitudes, desires, actions, and their capacity to do evil.

Question 4 It is impossible to escape the presence of God, for he can find us anywhere (vv. 7–12). God is omnipresent in that we cannot get away from his presence. To those who sometimes feel that God has abandoned them, this truth is of great comfort because they are not alone even though they may feel lonely.

Question 5 Some biblical examples are Jonah, Ananias and Sapphira (Acts 5), and Achan (Joshua 7). Sin is the only thing that would prompt a person to want to flee from God. The prophet Jonah is a good example of one who thought he could run away from God by hiding in the hull of a ship bound in the opposite direction from which he had been directed to go. He learned otherwise.

Likewise, Ananias and Sapphira discovered that they could not conspire together to lie to the Holy Spirit. Achan learned that he could not hide anything in his tent that would escape the notice of God. We cannot hide from God regardless of our spiritual state, geographical location, or status in life.

Question 6 The power of God is illustrated, not in a detached and abstract way, but in the formation of our bodies. God stitched us together while we were in the womb. (The word for "unformed body" [v. 16] can also be translated "embryo.") God's omnipotence, then, is his power to effect everything and anything that has been made or done or that could possibly be made or done in the universe.

Question 7 The fact that God knew us and entered into a loving relationship with us while we were still mere muscle, sinew, flesh, and bones coming together in the uterus of our mothers indicates that he regarded us as persons long before we were born, long before we had done anything, and long before we worried about our self-worth and esteem. That tells us a great deal as to whether a fetus constitutes a person. God regarded us as persons while we were embryos!

Question 8 If God saw us in the womb and ordained all our days before one of them had come to pass (v. 16), there is no reason to doubt that each person has an enormous amount of self-esteem and worth simply because God set the standard long before we were even born. Worth comes because we were loved by God before we were born and because we were made in the image of God.

Study Five

Worshiping the Holy King of Glory
Psalm 24

Purpose   To help us prepare for worship of God, through self-examination, in anticipation of his rule and reign.

Question 2   Verse 4 states that we can only truly enter into the worship of God when we are clean and pure. That is possible solely because God has graciously provided a way for sinful men and women to come before him on the basis of his righteousness, not their own. Ultimately, only the truly Righteous One, the Lord Jesus, could ever stand before the Father as completely pure. All others must borrow righteousness from him according to the means provided by Jesus' sacrificial death.

Question 3   Psalms 93:1 and 96:10 connect these concepts with the truth that the Lord is King. Therefore, the question is not simply, "Who is able to enter the temple gates to worship God?" More important, the question of the psalm is, "Who is able to stand before the *holy God* who is the King of Glory?"

Question 4   God looked at the hearts of the two brothers Cain and Abel, who came to sacrifice, before he looked at their offerings (Genesis 4:1–7). Samuel likewise had to instruct King Saul that obedience was preferred to sacrifice (1 Samuel 15:22). God always looks at our hearts first and then at the solo we sing, the money we bring, or the sermon to which we cling.

Question 5   Almost the same question is posed in Psalm 15:1 as in Psalm 24:1. The basic issues in Psalm 15 include the person who is blameless in lifestyle, righteous in deeds, truthful in speech, honorable with the neighbor, right in values, faithful to one's promises, concerned for the weak, and generous with the poor. This is a list of positive values based on the instruction, or Torah, of God's word for all who would wish to dwell in God's house or live on his holy hill.

Question 6 The concept of "blessing" and "vindication"—or as it is translated in other texts, "righteousness"—appears frequently in the Beatitudes. Both the Beatitudes and Psalm 24 describe what it means to live life under the rule of God.

Question 7 "Seeking God's face" is best understood by Jacob's experience at Peniel (Genesis 32:24–32), where he wrestled with the Lord (called the Angel of the Lord). Jacob would not let him go until he had received a blessing. This interpretation is to be preferred over a mere physical seeing of God's face, which Moses was specifically told was impossible for any person to experience and still live (Exodus 33:17–23). Matthew 5:8 says that only those who are pure in the realm of the heart will be able to "see God." Surely this, too, refers to spiritual rather than physical perception.

Question 8 The Messiah came to Jerusalem riding on a colt on Palm Sunday. The crowds enthusiastically welcomed him as a king and begged him to "save now, save now, Hosanna."

Question 9 The King of Glory will come once more at his second advent. Revelation 19:11–16 describes how he will enter the earthly scene and strike down the nations. He will be acclaimed and seen for who he is: "King of kings and Lord of lords."

Study
Six
Praying Out of the Depths of Our Sinfulness
Psalm 130

Purpose To gain the assurance that when we cry out to God in despair and defeat, he stands ready to grant forgiveness, grace, and redemption.

Question 2 When we forgive another person, it entails a willingness to personally bear the debt that the person owes us, whether it is material, verbal, or emotional. It is impossible to forgive without paying whatever the offending person owes. What makes forgiveness difficult is the human tendency to require others to pay the price for their wrongdoing. Because we may act that way toward our fellowmen, we tend to think that God might have the same attitude toward us. Therefore we are hesitant to come to him and ask for the forgiveness he freely offers.

Question 3 "Out of the depths" may refer to any threat or danger that we face, such as a life-threatening illness or condition, a recurring fear or phobia, the hostility of people who are important to us, a tragedy, or a spiritual problem with which we are wrestling.

Question 4 No matter how desperate the situation, we are never out of the earshot of God. The psalmist was convinced that in spite of the gravity of his own situation, God was not far off, nor was he unresponsive. More often than not, it is only during tragic events that people or nations learn to finally cry out to God when he has otherwise been avoided.

Often Israel had to fall into desperate straits before the nation would finally pay attention to her spiritual needs. During Pharaoh's oppression just before the Exodus, Israel cried to the Lord (Exodus 3:7, 9). Yet nothing can separate us from the love of God (Romans 8:38–39).

Question 5 God is totally aware of all our sin, for he knows everything. And we all have sinned (Romans 3:23). This raises the question of how anyone can dare to approach him or even hope to stand in his presence. If God were ever to demand a complete accounting for our sin, we would all be in real trouble. However, in spite of what he knows about us, he is willing to forgive us freely and graciously.

Question 6 The three fundamental characteristics set forth by the preposition "with" are forgiveness (v. 4), steadfast love or grace (v. 7), and full or great redemption (v. 7). All three find their source in God and are here described as his intimate friends and companions. The unique word for "forgiveness" is used only with God as its subject. In Hebrew it is used with an article—*the* forgiveness—and denotes the payment we need to become free of our load of sin and the depths in which we are mired. His "steadfast love," or "unfailing love," also uses the article in Hebrew; the word appears 248 times in the Old Testament. It means divine grace offered freely, based on God's own promise to be loyal and faithful to what he offered as a gift. Finally, God offers his "full" or "great" redemption, which fulfills his personal promise to ransom and deliver all who need to be released from the bonds of sin and self.

Question 7 In the Bible, hope is never a matter of luck or pure chance, as if we said, "I hope that such and such will happen."

Instead it is a solid confidence and a certainty that the God who stands behind his word will be vindicated and proven trustworthy. It is this kind of hope that we hold with more intense anticipation than that with which sentries wait for the night to pass and the shadows of darkness to give way to the light of morning. This image of the sentry or watchman carries a double function: (a) the all-night vigil ends when the morning light breaks, and (b) the threat that accompanies the darkness is also relieved when the dawn appears.

Note that Isaiah 40:31 likewise teaches that those who wait on the Lord are precisely the same group who have their strength renewed.

Question 8   The two objects of hope are (a) the Lord, and (b) his word (v. 5). If we wait for circumstances, other people, world conditions, or anything else to improve, we delude ourselves. Our generation has typically put its trust in education, money, influence, power, or other things. All these are transitory and changing, so we need to return to the dependability of God's Word and the uniqueness of his person if we are to have any hope for the future.

Question 9   God will surely forgive all who call to him in despair, but he has much more in store for them. His grace and love will follow them all the days of their lives (v. 7). Moreover, their redemption will be completed and declared "full" when Christ returns to earth. Romans 8:20 and following declares that the whole created order will shout with joy as his reappearance signals the restoration of the created order to its original condition. What joy there will be in that "full" redemption!

Question 10   The access to God that the psalmist found when he turned to him in despair is denied to no one. There is always an open line to the Father, and he invites all his children to seek his face daily. We need to be faithful in praying not only for our own concerns, but that evil might be handicapped all over the world. We need to pray for all kinds of Christian ministries, both locally and around the world. We are to use prayer for more than just an emergency number for contacting God when we are in distress. We are to bring every part of life under the covering of prayer.

Confessing Our Transgressions
Psalms 51 and 32

Purpose To help us remember and experience the wonderful grace of God and the forgiveness he offers to all who confess their transgressions.

Question 1 Unfortunately, sin continues to pervade the human situation. The truth is that few, if any, of us ever learn all we should from the sins and mistakes of the past. This may be foolish, but we insist on having our own way. Perhaps no sin, despite more than enough lessons from the past, has cursed the present generation as much as the sin of infidelity to one's marriage partner. We are prone to rationalize and try to justify this conduct even though God has condemned such promiscuity in the severest terms in Scripture.

Question 2 The psalmist appeals to three of God's attributes: his mercy, his unfailing love, and his compassion. These are the same three qualities of God found in Exodus 34:6–7. As always, it is God's character, not human sinfulness, that must be at the heart of the story to forgive. If God were not such a loving and merciful God, where could sinners go to find relief from their shame and guilt?

Question 3 Failure to confess our sin before God results in severe physical, emotional, and spiritual consequences. It will do no good to try to forget about our sins or to hope that the memories and feelings of guilt will pass over. They will not! David felt as if his bones would burst and the very sap of his vitality would be drained from his body during the days when he refused to confess his sin to God (see Psalm 34:3–4). Hiding our sin from God is not only useless, but also counterproductive to our health, spiritual well-being, and enjoyment of life.

Question 4 David came to three conclusions about his sin: (a) his sin offended God, and therefore God was altogether justified in his judgment against him; (b) he needed to acknowledge it and stop covering up, for it could not be hidden, and he was finding no relief in spirit, soul, or body; and (c) he recognized that he had been a sinner from his birth, for his depravity could be traced back even to his time in the womb (v. 5). These conclusions are universal principles that still apply to all.

Question 5   Cleansing in the Old Testament was not just an external matter. It had to take place in the "inner parts" (v. 6), the "inmost place" (v. 6), and "within me" (v. 10). God had to "create . . . a pure heart" and "renew a steadfast spirit" in David (v. 10).

Question 6   Compare this text with 1 Samuel 15:22 and Isaiah 1:11–18. God is not denying that sacrifices are useful or even commanded by him; his point is that sacrifice when there is unconfessed sin in our lives is empty ritual. Sacrifice in and of itself is neither pleasing nor displeasing to God. Rather, it is a right attitude of heart and a sincere confession that make a sacrifice worthy. This point is repeated time and again in the Old Testament—for example, in 1 Samuel 15:22; Isaiah 1:11–18; Jeremiah 7:21–22; Hosea 6:6; and Micah 6:8.

Question 7   The verb "to create" (Hebrew: *bara*) appears forty-five times in the Old Testament, with God as the verb's only subject. There is no agency of material when this word is used, indicating that everything God creates is brand-new and comes directly from his hand. Therefore, it is surprising to find this verb used in verse 10 to refer to God's activity in creating a new thing in David. So radical was David's cleansing that he was like a brand-new baby. He was reborn in his heart as he was purged of his sin and guilt. God saw that David's spirit was broken and his heart contrite (v. 17), and therefore he created in him a "pure heart" and a "steadfast spirit."

Question 8   After the sinner has experienced such marvelous grace from the Lord, he is so motivated by this relief of spirit and soul that he offers now to "teach transgressors [God's] ways" so that "sinners will turn back to [God]." The same connection exists in Psalm 32:8, although there the psalmist notes that he must first be instructed by God before he can teach others. In a similar manner, we who are forgiven so much are called to "make disciples of all nations, . . . teaching them to obey everything [God] has commanded" (Matthew 28:20).

Question 9   David urges us not to be as dull and slow to respond to the promptings of the Holy Spirit and the teaching of God as he was. A horse needs a bit and bridle in order to be steered and led. But humans should not be so stupid and slow to heed the call of God that they need such pieces of equipment for guidance and direction.

Unforgiven persons find it impossible to know the will of God. But forgiven persons can be taught to instruct others about the wonderful grace, compassion, and mercy of God.

Study Eight   *The Lord Is Present*
Psalms 23 and 46

Purpose   To learn that when God is truly our Shepherd, we have everything and lack nothing; and that his presence will sustain us even if the world—or our world—is falling apart.

Question 2   God is and remains the only necessity of life, for he is able to provide all the things we consider necessary to life: food, drink, shelter, protection, relationship. Often what we think we need turns out to be a toy we soon discard. If only we would seek first the Lord and his righteousness, we would find that everything else falls into place (Matthew 6:33).

Question 3   The imagery of green pastures, quiet waters, and inner restoration is not primarily a picture of pastoral peace and rural tranquillity. Rather, it affirms that God provides food ("green pastures") and drink ("still waters"). Sheep will not drink from a stream where the water is flowing rapidly. On the "right paths" we avoid holes and pits that would cause injury or cause us to stumble, and we do not fall prey to wild animals. "Restoring the soul" can be understood as "keeping us alive."

Just as sheep owe their preservation to the shepherd, so we owe our preservation to God, who keeps on providing us all that we need. This may sound like a naive platitude when we are faced by severe crises—terrorism, proliferation of nuclear weapons, ecological problems, or worldwide economic uncertainty—but we are told not to worry. If we seek the Lord and his kingdom, everything else we need will be provided, including a sense of security.

Question 4   God's presence is able to counter even the most life-threatening situations, including death itself. Central to the whole psalm is the affirmation in verse 4: "You are with me." The Shepherd is more than a match for evil in all its forms. The power of God may be a threat to those who oppose him, but it is a comfort to those who are part of his family.

Question 5 God's *love* in this passage is the beautiful Hebrew word *hesed*, which is used 248 times in the Old Testament and translated variously as "loving-kindness," "loyal fidelity," "covenantal love," and "grace." No single or even compound English word can capture all that this Hebrew word embodies. It was first introduced as a description of God's character in Exodus 34:6–7.

God's *goodness* celebrates the totality of his attributes in their perfection. Thus it was that God caused all his "goodness" to "pass by" in front of his discouraged servant Moses in Exodus 33:19 and before his despondent servant Elijah in 1 Kings 19:11. Everything God is and stands for can be called his "goodness." Therefore, both his love and his goodness will literally "chase" us throughout life. To "follow" is not a mere tagging along behind, but connotes pursuing those who keep running away from his presence—erroneously thinking they can make it through life on their own without God's presence, love, and goodness.

Question 6 To take refuge in the Lord is to depend on him alone. Consequently, it does not matter how severe the crisis or even if the world is about to fall apart. We can take refuge in God, for he alone can give life and immortality. Any of our worst-case scenarios will not affect this truth: God will remain our "refuge," "strength," and "help in [times of] trouble."

Question 7 This admonition is a summons to stop our routine activity and contemplate who God is. Often children are told in church to "be still," meaning "don't move." That meaning fits fairly well here.

Question 9 God's works know no limits other than those imposed by his own righteousness and consistency. He can—and he will— make the desolations that men set loose on planet earth to cease (v. 8). He will also bring a sudden halt to all wars and all the weapons of warfare (v. 9). He will do this when he returns the second time. The best places in Scripture to see this glorious picture of the future are Zechariah 14 and Revelation 21 and 22.

On the Edge of Unbelief
Psalm 73

Purpose   To see the affairs and prosperity of the wicked from our own perspective that regards the sovereignty of God, his care for his people, and his reign for all eternity.

Question 2   The Bible clearly rejects any suggestion that those who love the Lord will be rich, healthy, and generally prosperous. There is no guaranteed formula of naming and claiming all we want. From our own experience and from Scripture we observe many whom God loved, yet who endured great suffering and trials. For example, Abel, Job, Hosea, the widow women who helped Elijah and Elisha. Therefore, prosperity is not necessarily a sign of God's approval, nor is suffering necessarily a sign of God's disapproval.

Question 3   Verse 1 functions as the title to the whole psalm and is perhaps a summary of what the writer has learned as a result of his experience: God is good to his people, and no matter how much the wicked may seem to prosper in this life, when the story is finished and history comes to a close, God's people will know his eternal blessing and the wicked will receive the judgment they deserve.

Question 4   The wicked seem to be
— Without any struggles (v. 4a)
— Healthy and strong in body (v. 4b)
— Free from the burdens of other mortals (v. 5a)
— Untouched by ills common to other humans (v. 5b)
— Proud (v. 6)
— Violent (v. 6b)
— Callous by nature and in heart (v. 7a)
— Limitless in their conceit (v. 7b)
— Scoffers (v. 8a)
— Oppressive (8b)
— Possessive of everything (v. 9)
— Carefree
This is an accurate description of many of the ungodly in our day, just as it is for all of history.

Question 5   The effect on the faithful is to tempt them to doubt that God noticed their plight. There seems to be no stopping the wicked, for everything they touch appears to turn to gold (v. 10). Their arrogance is mocking: "How can God know?" They surmise that God has no knowledge of what we do, and therefore we can do as we please. This notion affects the psalmist so much that he throws up his hands in disgust and defeat and concludes, "[It has all been] in vain" (v. 13). He feels that his efforts to keep his heart pure and innocent have all been to no avail.

We, of course, can be affected by the same logic if we take our eyes off the Lord and look only at our circumstances.

Question 6   The change comes for the psalmist when he enters God's house, hears God's Word proclaimed, and gets his priorities straightened out. He sees what would happen in the end when these arrogant sinners face the God they regard as blind to their thoughts and conduct. The wicked are on a slippery slope because they will ultimately come to ruin if they remain on their evil path.

The image of a dream in verse 20 is very striking.

Question 7   He is ashamed of his bizarre behavior expressed in verses 21–22. His heart has been grieved and his spirit made bitter by what he thought was an unanswerable problem for God. Now, however, he sees that he had been "senseless," "ignorant," and little more than "a brute beast" (v. 22). We exhibit the same attitude when we lose our perspective on God.

Job is a clear example of this attitude. He was reminded of these truths when he began to doubt God during all his troubles. When God finally dealt with him, Job meekly concluded that he had "spoken of things he did not understand, things too wonderful for him to know" (Job 42:3).

Question 9   The hope of the psalmist is to be joined to God in glory after death. Since he will be with God in heaven, there is nothing on earth he prefers or desires in addition to God (vv. 24b–25). The hope of heaven and assurance of a resurrection are clearly taught in the Old Testament.

Study Ten

Coming to Terms with Time
Psalm 90

Purpose   To take account of our use of time and the abilities that God has given us, and to regard each day as a gift from him.

Question 1   God is not arbitrary or capricious. Whether we live a short life or a long life, God is still God. Every moment is a gift from God, not an entitlement, because he made us for himself.

Question 2   The implication of the verbs "were born" and "brought forth" is that God is before all matter and all time; he is eternal. Therefore everything in the world depends on God, for he is from "everlasting to everlasting."

Question 3   Even though different Hebrew words are translated "dust" in Genesis 3:19 and Psalm 90:3, the point of our mortality and vulnerability is easily recognized. Before God blew into him the "breath of life," man was not "alive." The word *dust* in this passage means something like "crushed particles." That is what our bodies will become when we die. This truth serves to give us a healthy perspective on who we are and who God is.

Question 4   Because God is outside of time, he reckons a thousand years as little more than a day, or "a watch in the night" (v. 4). But from the human standpoint, time can seem to drag on interminably or speed by so fast that everything becomes a blur. God is everlasting and is not subject to the problems of time that we mortals face.

Question 5   Our "secret sins" and "iniquities" have provoked God's wrath. Moses' iniquity was to imply that he could bring water out of the rock for the thirsty Israelites. See Psalm 106:32–33.

Even though, as God's great mediator, Moses had rescued the children of Israel three times by his prayers, he now prayed that God would let him lead Israel into the Promised Land, and God denied his request.

Question 6   The psalmist is asking for the wisdom to accept the days and time given from the hand of God. From this knowledge, the "wise heart" no longer fusses over how many days it has, but instead turns to using each one to the honor and glorify God.

Question 7   Compare Moses' request of God in Exodus 32:12 and God's response in Exodus 32:14; 34:6–7. Rather than asking God to change the duration of a person's life, Moses is seeking forgiveness of sins—the very roadblocks that initially raised the issue of physical and spiritual death. Only when God forgives us can the gulf between us and the Lord be bridged. That was the same request that

Moses made when Israel had sinned by making the golden calf (Exodus 32). The Lord "relented" because of his nature, which Moses describes in Exodus 34 as "compassionate," "gracious," "slow to anger," and "abounding in love and faithfulness."

Question 8 God is unchanging in terms of his nature and character. That is why he must often "relent," "repent," or "change" in his actions when men and women change in their response to him. God is not frozen and immobile because of his unchanging character. On the contrary, he alters his attitude and regard toward mortals who change so that he might be consistent with his character and remain unchanging.

Question 9 Instead of our days being burdensome or another reminder of our mortality, we can be satisfied because we count on the faithfulness of God and not on our own abilities. It is God's "unfailing love" (the very aspect of God's character that Moses was taught in Exodus 34:6–7) that makes life livable. God redeems time because he redeems mortals who live in time and then pursues those mortals all the days of their lives with "goodness" and "love." This is very different from "positive thinking"—when people merely emphasize the positive and try to forget the negative. Even counseling, as helpful and useful as it may be, cannot begin to compare with the matchless grace, love, faithfulness, and mercy that a personal heavenly Father bestows on all who come to him in faith.

Question 10 Because God is eternally faithful and everlasting in reign and authority, our work and our lives can take on a meaning that they otherwise would not have. In these verses we are called to entrust ourselves, our time, our labor, and our children to God.

Study
Eleven

Standing Beneath the Cross of Jesus
Psalm 22

Purpose To see Jesus as the suffering psalmist, and to know that because of his suffering on the cross, he is with us in all our times of crisis and pain.

Question 3 God is enthroned not only in the temple, but also on the praises of his people. Therefore, the praise we offer to God in the congregation of the righteous must come from our hearts and lips. Praise is not an optional part of a worship service, nor is it part of the so-called preliminaries. The choruses and the hymns cannot be cheap, shallow, or boring, because God is the great King. Also, our singing must not be used to exhibit our abilities and turn the focus on us and away from God.

Consider singing one of the praise hymns or choruses at this point in the study.

Question 4 The introduction to this study gives us a head start. Some comparisons:

> — The crowd hurled insults at Jesus as he hung on the cross.
> — They unwittingly used the very words of Scripture to mock Jesus: "He trusts in God. Let God rescue him now if he wants him."
> — Jesus was "pierced" (v. 16) by one of the soldiers using a spear.
> — Jesus' garments were divided by the soldiers who crucified him, and they cast lots for his clothing (v. 18).

Both the crowd and the Roman soldiers were unwitting accomplices to the fullfillment of the Old Testament scriptures. Although they were probably ignorant of what God's Word said, the Lord ironically used them to confirm that Word.

Question 5 Jesus had a virgin birth, so he is always connected in Scripture with a human mother, but not a human father. Moreover, his mother is twice identified in these verses as the begetter of the Messiah, but never in association with a father.

Question 6 The sufferer prays for (a) God's presence, (b) God's help, and (c) God's deliverance from the sword, the dogs, lions, and bulls or wild oxen. Anyone who claims that the Father failed to answer this prayer of Jesus should reflect on the fact that God answered more mightily than merely delivering him from the immediate peril or danger: He raised Jesus from the dead! This is mightier than all other forms of deliverance hoped for, for it demonstrated the power, authority, and ultimate triumph of God in a most spectacular way.

Question 7   At this point the suffering psalmist shifts the focus from his agony to the goodness and grace of the Lord. Even amid pain and struggle, there is still room to praise God.

Question 9   The significance of these three declarations of completion in history are that they marked

— The end of God's work in creation and the beginning of his work in providence (Genesis 1:31)
— The end of his promise to provide salvation and his actual work of providing it (John 19:30)
— The separation between history and eternity (Revelation 21:6)

Walking Around Zion
Psalms 48 and 122

Purpose   To have the assurance of God's presence and security, and to experience the peace and unity that should characterize the people of God.

Question 2   The physical splendor of the city reminds the writer of the glory of God, who has shown his presence there. As the city is lofty, so is God, the great King, high above on his throne (see Psalm 122:5), where he rules and watches over us. God has revealed himself through his many acts in behalf of the city and its people.

Question 3   The events that come to mind might include the siege by Sennacherib (2 Kings 18:13; 19:32–36). The reference to "ships of Tarshish"—that is, Phoenicia, a strong seafaring nation—recalls the bold and confident enemies that surrounded the land of the Israelites and proposed a perpetual and not-too-distant threat.

But the city's security rested in the plans and purposes of God, not its strong walls and military defenses. Jerusalem has played a key role in history, and nothing can happen to the city that does not advance God's purposes.

Question 4   "Praise" connotes the glory, holiness, and majesty of God, while the "right hand" connotes justice, power, and authority. The concepts form a contrast, but they are not contradictory; they are different ways of looking at God, who has all these attributes, and more.

Question 5 The verbs, of course, are *walk, go around, count, consider,* and *view.* The physical evidence of the defenses of the city reminds us of how God has protected his people. We are admonished to teach this knowledge to our families and descendants, in this passage and in the many other places in Scripture (such as Deuteronomy 6:4–8).

Question 7 Many concepts are expressed in both psalms, such as the lofty splendor of the city, its citadel and fortifications, the feelings of rejoicing and praise to God, and God's justice. However, the psalms are not so much repetitious as they are complementary; together they form a lavish song of God's care for his people.

CPSIA information can be obtained
at www.ICGtesting.com
Printed in the USA
LVHW03s2242300818
588569LV00001B/1/P